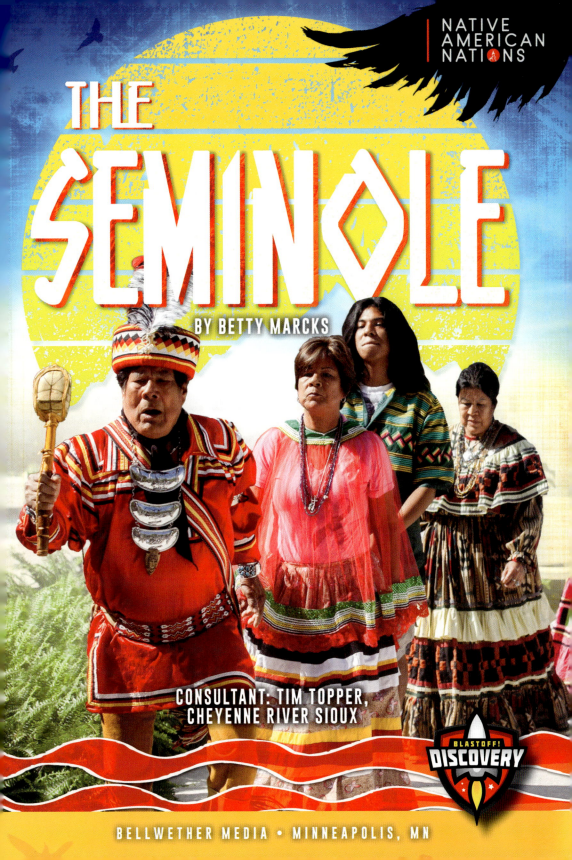

Blastoff! Discovery launches a new mission: reading to learn. Filled with facts and features, each book offers you an exciting new world to explore!

Author's Statement of Positionality:
I am a white woman of European descent. As such, I can claim no direct lived experience of being a Native American. In writing this book, I have tried to be an ally by relying on sources by Native American writers and authors whenever possible and have worked to let their voices guide its content.

This edition first published in 2026 by Bellwether Media, Inc.

No part of this publication may be reproduced in whole or in part without written permission of the publisher.
For information regarding permission, write to Bellwether Media, Inc.,
Attention: Permissions Department,
3500 American Blvd W, Suite 150, Bloomington, MN 55431.

Library of Congress Cataloging-in-Publication Data

LC record for The Seminole available at: https://lccn.loc.gov/2025018379

Text copyright © 2026 by Bellwether Media, Inc. BLASTOFF! DISCOVERY and associated logos are trademarks and/or registered trademarks of Bellwether Media, Inc. Bellwether Media is a division of FlutterBee Education Group.

Editor: Elizabeth Neuenfeldt   Series Designer: Andrea Schneider
Book Designer: Laura Sowers

Printed in the United States of America, North Mankato, MN.

TABLE OF CONTENTS

ONE NATION OUT OF MANY	4
TRADITIONAL SEMINOLE LIFE	6
EUROPEAN CONTACT	12
LIFE TODAY	16
CONTINUING TRADITIONS	20
FIGHT TODAY, BRIGHT TOMORROW	24
TIMELINE	28
GLOSSARY	30
TO LEARN MORE	31
INDEX	32

ONE NATION OUT OF MANY

The Seminole are **descendants** of many Native American nations. The nations include the Timucua, Calusa, Tequesta, Ais, Jeaga, Apalachee, and Miccosukee. Their homelands cover today's Florida, Georgia, Alabama, South Carolina, Tennessee, and Mississippi. These nations lived as separate groups for thousands of years.

Europeans arrived starting around 1500. They spread diseases and took over land. The many Native American nations of the southeastern United States came together. They fought for their lands and ways of life. Survivors moved into Florida. **Colonizers** in the area began to call them Seminoles.

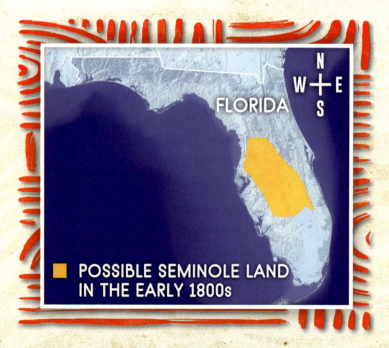

POSSIBLE SEMINOLE LAND IN THE EARLY 1800s

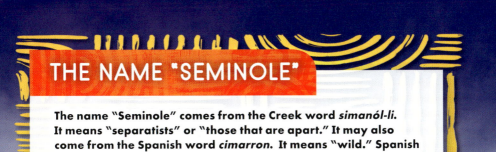

THE NAME "SEMINOLE"

The name "Seminole" comes from the Creek word *simanól-li*. It means "separatists" or "those that are apart." It may also come from the Spanish word *cimarron*. It means "wild." Spanish colonizers used this word to refer to ancestral Seminole people.

TRADITIONAL SEMINOLE LIFE

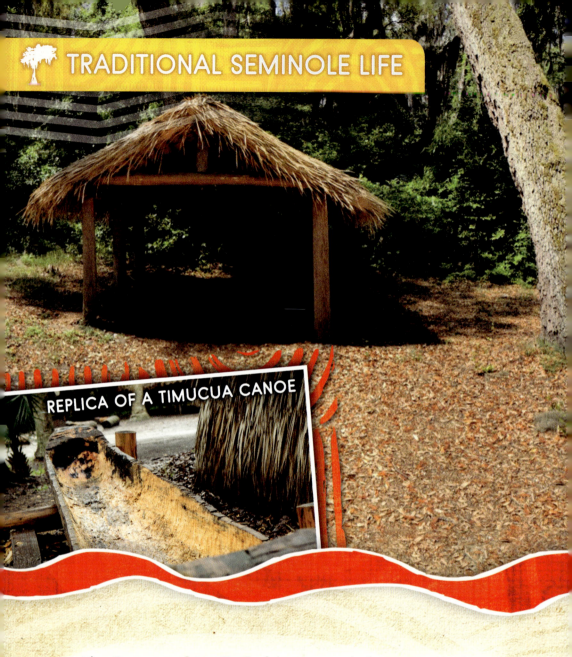

REPLICA OF A TIMUCUA CANOE

The **Ancestral Period** of the Seminole began more than 14,000 years ago in northern Florida. The earliest ancestors mostly lived near the coastlines throughout the **Ice Age**. People moved farther into the **peninsula** as the Ice Age ended. Some groups began farming.

REPLICAS OF TIMUCUA HOMES

Different nations grew throughout the peninsula. Each nation had its own **traditions** and **cultures**. Many communities did well and became large sites. These sites were part of a trade system. It spanned north to the **Great Lakes**.

EARTHWORK MOUND

The people started to change the land as they developed settlements. Earthwork mounds were human-made structures that some ancestral Seminole created. The mounds kept communities safe from changing water levels. They also acted as important areas for **ceremonies**, travel, and trade.

Nations across the peninsula built many kinds of homes. But ancestral Seminoles needed to be able to flee quickly from U.S. troops in the 1800s. They created *chickees*. These homes are made of logs and leaves. They are quick to build and take down.

MOUND MATERIALS

Some ancestral earthwork mounds had sea shells as a base. Sand and earth were layered on top of the shells.

SEMINOLE RESOURCES

PALMETTO

CYPRESS LOGS

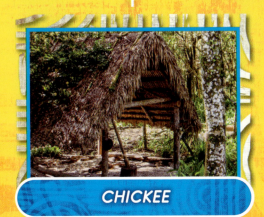

CHICKEE

Clans are an important part of Seminole society. A person with a Seminole mother becomes a member of her clan. Every person within a clan is family. Members of clans are expected to follow rules. Individuals must marry a person outside of their clan. A husband joins his wife's clan.

There are eight Seminole clans. All clans are equal. They hold different strengths, such as courage. A clan ends when the last female of the clan passes on.

EIGHT CLANS

The eight clans include Panther, Bear, Deer, Wind, Bigtown, Bird, Snake, and Otter.

EUROPEAN CONTACT

ILLUSTRATION OF CALUSA PEOPLE DEFENDING THEIR HOME

Spain wanted to claim the Florida Peninsula around 1500. At first, the Calusa forced the Spanish out. But the Spanish returned. They brought deadly diseases to ancestral Seminole. The diseases and conflicts caused by Europeans led to extreme loss of life for the ancestors.

The ancestors that survived came together. They created a new culture and way of life. The Seminole formed towns and farms by 1800. They were successful ranchers.

FREEDOM IN FLORIDA

Some Black people who escaped slavery fled to Florida. The Seminole welcomed them into their communities.

CATTLE ON BIG CYPRESS SEMINOLE INDIAN RESERVATION

U.S. troops invaded Seminole lands in 1817. The U.S. government forced the Seminole to sign a **treaty** in 1823. It demanded they move to a **reservation** in central Florida. Troops attacked again in 1835. The Seminoles held them off for seven years. But there was a great amount of loss. Thousands of Seminole people were forced west. Fewer than 500 remained in the southern **Everglades**.

FAMOUS SEMINOLE

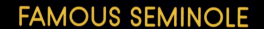

ASI-YAHOLA (OSCEOLA)

BIRTHDAY 1804

DEATH January 30, 1838

FAMOUS FOR

A skillful speaker and warrior who led Seminole warriors during conflicts with the U.S.

TREE OF TEARS, A SEMINOLE BURIAL SITE FROM THE 1838 BATTLE OF LOXAHATCHEE

The U.S. began a third major conflict in 1855. It tried to force the remaining Seminole people west. Many were forced out, but some stayed hidden in the Everglades.

15

LIFE TODAY

Today, the Seminole nation is made up of three tribes. The Seminole Nation of Oklahoma's government is in Wewoka, Oklahoma. The Tribe has around 18,800 members. The Seminole Tribe of Florida is in Hollywood, Florida. It has more than 5,000 members. The Miccosukee Tribe of Indians of Florida is in the Tamiami Trail Reservation. It serves around 640 members.

Members of the Seminole nation live and work on tribal lands. Many live throughout the U.S. and the rest of the world, too. People do all types of work. Some work in schools and hospitals. Others own businesses.

SEMINOLE CULTURE CLASS AT THE BIG CYPRESS SEMINOLE INDIAN RESERVATION

WEWOKA, OKLAHOMA

Seminole Tribes serve members of their communities. The tribes are led by either a General **Council** or Tribal Council. Council members are responsible for maintaining the government of their tribe.

GOVERNMENT OF THE SEMINOLE TRIBE OF FLORIDA

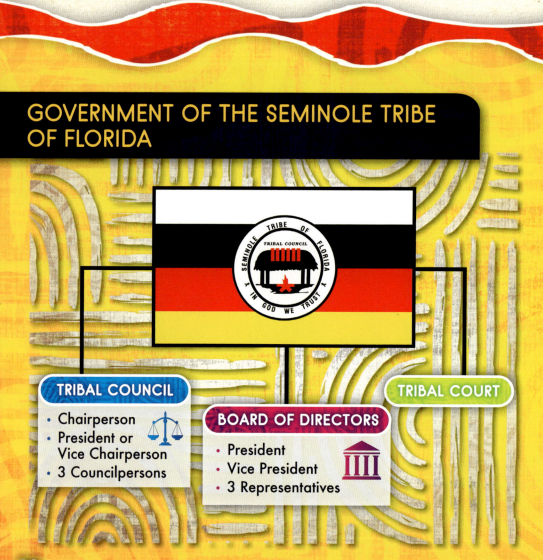

TRIBAL COUNCIL
- Chairperson
- President or Vice Chairperson
- 3 Councilpersons

BOARD OF DIRECTORS
- President
- Vice President
- 3 Representatives

TRIBAL COURT

SEMINOLE HARD ROCK HOTEL & CASINO

The tribes provide services to their members. These include education, housing, police and fire services, and much more. The services keep members safe and healthy. All three tribes own and run casinos. The Seminole Tribe of Florida has popular **tourism** businesses.

CONTINUING TRADITIONS

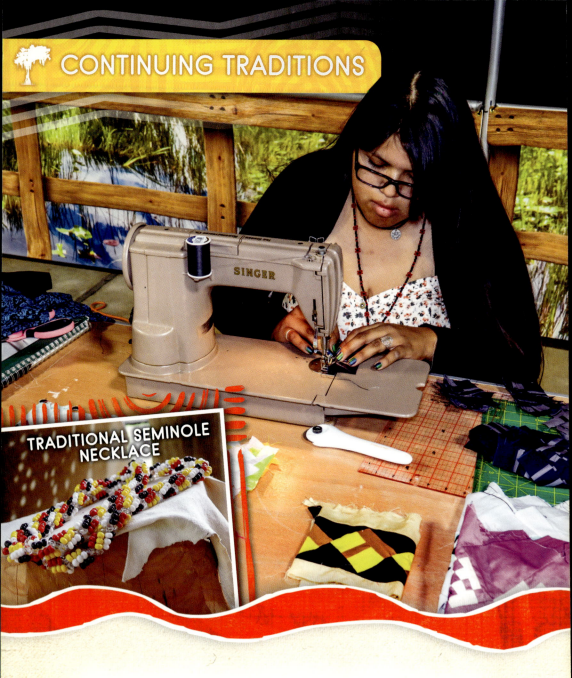

TRADITIONAL SEMINOLE NECKLACE

Some Seminole practice the traditions of their ancestors. Traditional clothing and accessories are bold and colorful. Beaded necklaces and bandolier bags feature detailed designs. It may take up to two years to make a bandolier bag.

Trading posts ended by the 1900s. Many Seminole were affected economically. Patchwork became a common clothing style around the 1910s. Creating clothing from patches of cloth became a necessity. It has grown into a popular style. Today, patchwork designs are detailed. They showcase many different skills and styles.

TRADITIONAL BANDOLIER BAGS

Ancestral Seminole men used bandolier bags to hold important items such as tobacco. The bags are traditionally made of wool. They include beaded designs that may stand for clans, animals, or different meanings.

Cowkeeping has been a part of Seminole culture since the early 1500s. The Calusa were the first to keep cattle. Today, Florida Seminole ranchers use traditional knowledge and modern ranching practices to help their businesses grow.

The Seminole have a long history with alligators. Their ancestors hunted alligators. They later traded alligator hides. Today, alligator wrestling is a show of respect for the animal and what it has provided to the Seminole.

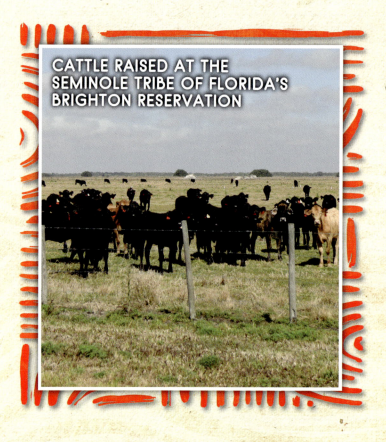

CATTLE RAISED AT THE SEMINOLE TRIBE OF FLORIDA'S BRIGHTON RESERVATION

KEEPING THEIR LANGUAGE

The Seminole Nation of Oklahoma's Language Preservation Program helps members learn Mvskoke. They offer online courses, audio recordings of picture books, social events, and more.

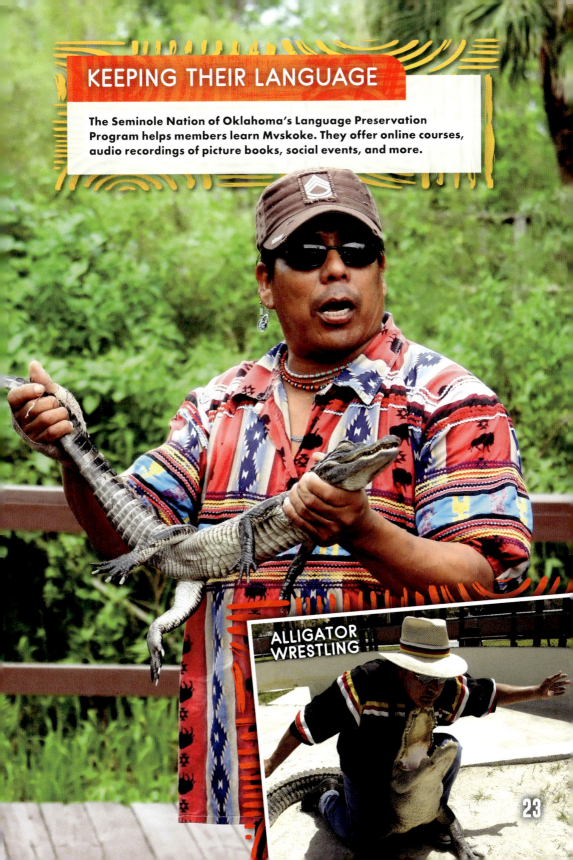

ALLIGATOR WRESTLING

FIGHT TODAY, BRIGHT TOMORROW

TINA OSCEOLA

White people have harmed Native American peoples throughout history. One way is through grave robbing. White people have dug up Native American graves to steal cultural items and human remains. Some museums were developed as places to keep them.

The Smithsonian Museum of Natural History holds 1,500 remains of Seminole ancestors. Tina Osceola is head of the Seminole Tribe of Florida's Tribal Historic **Preservation** Office. She has been working for over 10 years to get ancestors' remains back. Holding remains of their ancestors in museums deeply goes against traditional Seminole beliefs. The Seminole believe their ancestors cannot be at rest.

NAGPRA

The Native American Graves Protection and Repatriation Act (NAGPRA) is a federal law. It helps museums return Native American remains and cultural items. It makes sure Native American remains and cultural items are always treated with respect.

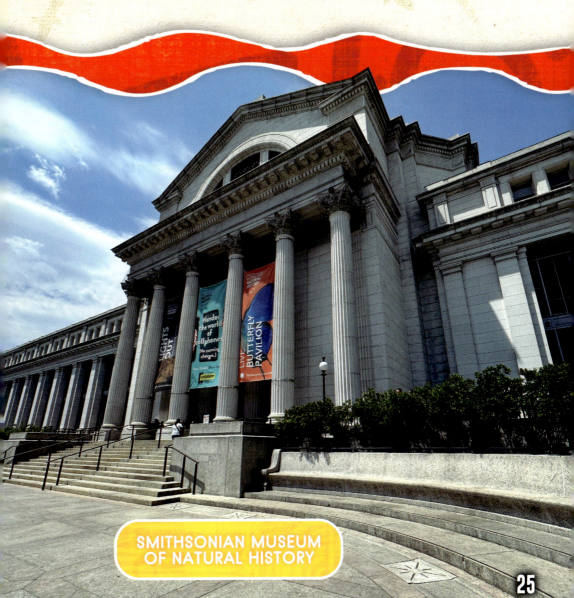

SMITHSONIAN MUSEUM OF NATURAL HISTORY

Climate change affects Seminole culture. Rising temperatures, major storms, flooding, and other weather events harm the land. The Seminole cannot get the natural resources they need to practice their culture. It is harder for them to practice their hunting, medicinal, and ceremonial traditions.

MARTHA TOMMIE, A MEMBER OF THE SEMINOLE TRIBE OF FLORIDA, RAISING AWARENESS ABOUT CLIMATE CHANGE

The Seminole Tribe of Florida's Climate Action Plan is a community-led effort to fight climate change. Elders, Tribal citizens, and technical staff work together to make a plan that will also be a model for other nations. Their efforts will protect the land for the future!

TIMELINE

AROUND 1500
The Calusa, ancestors of the Seminole, keep the Spanish from taking their lands

LATE 1770s
Colonizers begin using the name Seminole

1856
The Seminole Nation of Oklahoma becomes a federally recognized nation

1858
What are known by some as the Seminole Wars end

AROUND 1910
The Seminole create patchwork clothing

28

2011
Tina Osceola begins her efforts to get ancestral remains from the Smithsonian Museum of Natural History

1962
The Miccosukee Tribe of Indians of Florida becomes a federally recognized nation

1957
The Seminole Tribe of Florida becomes a federally recognized nation

2020
The Seminole Tribe of Florida starts a Climate Resiliency Program

1990
The Miccosukee Tribe opens the Miccosukee Indian Bingo Hall with high demand, leading to the opening of a resort and gaming facility nine years later

GLOSSARY

Ancestral Period—a time that began when the earliest Seminole people arrived in the Florida Peninsula and ended when colonizers arrived in the area

ceremonies—sets of actions performed in a particular way, often as part of religious or spiritual worship

clans—groups of people who share a common ancestor

climate change—a human-caused change in Earth's weather due to warming temperatures

colonizers—people who take control of a people or area

council—a group of people who meet to run a government

cultures—the beliefs, arts, and ways of life in places or societies

descendants—people related to a person or group of people who lived at an earlier time

Everglades—a large swamp region of southern Florida

Great Lakes—large freshwater lakes on the border between Canada and the United States; the Great Lakes are Superior, Michigan, Ontario, Erie, and Huron.

Ice Age—a period in Earth's history when the climate was much cooler and large areas of land were covered in sheets of ice

peninsula—a section of land that extends out from a larger piece of land and is almost completely surrounded by water

preservation—the process of keeping something in its original state

reservation—land set aside by the U.S. government for the forced removal of a Native American community from their original land

tourism—the business of people traveling to visit other places

traditions—customs, ideas, and beliefs handed down from one generation to the next

treaty—an official agreement between two groups

TO LEARN MORE

AT THE LIBRARY

Leaf, Christina. *Everglades National Park.* Minneapolis, Minn.: Bellwether Media, 2024.

Marcks, Betty. *The Muscogee.* Minneapolis, Minn.: Bellwether Media, 2025.

Sexton, Colleen. *Florida.* Minneapolis, Minn.: Bellwether Media, 2022.

ON THE WEB

FACTSURFER

Factsurfer.com gives you a safe, fun way to find more information.

1. Go to www.factsurfer.com.

2. Enter "the Seminole" into the search box and click 🔍.

3. Select your book cover to see a list of related content.

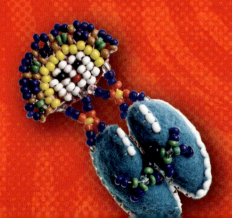

INDEX

Ais, 4
Apalachee, 4
Asi-Yahola, 14
bandolier bags, 20, 21
Calusa, 4, 12, 22
ceremonies, 8, 26
clans, 10, 11
Climate Action Plan, 27
climate change, 26, 27
councils, 18
culture, 4, 7, 8, 9, 12, 22, 23, 24, 25, 26
earthwork mounds, 8, 9
Everglades, 14, 15
future, 27
government of the Seminole Tribe of Florida, 18
history, 4, 5, 6, 7, 8, 9, 12, 13, 14, 15, 21, 22, 24
homelands, 4, 6, 7, 8, 12, 14, 15, 16, 26, 27
housing, 7, 8, 9
Jeaga, 4
language, 23
map, 4, 16
members, 16, 18, 19, 23, 27
Miccosukee, 4
Miccosukee Tribe of Indians of Florida, 16, 18, 19
name, 4, 5
Native American Graves Protection and Repatriation Act, 25
Osceola, Tina, 24
reservations, 13, 14, 16, 17, 22
Seminole Nation of Oklahoma, 16, 18, 19, 23
Seminole resources, 9
Seminole Tribe of Florida, 16, 18, 19, 22, 24, 27
Smithsonian Museum of Natural History, 24, 25
Tequesta, 4
timeline, 28–29
Timucua, 4, 6, 7
trade, 7, 8, 21, 22
traditions, 7, 8, 9, 10, 12, 20, 21, 22, 24, 26
U.S. government, 14, 15
U.S. troops, 8, 14

The images in this book are reproduced through the courtesy of: ZUMA Press Inc/ Alamy Stock Photo, front cover; Christine, pp. 3, 31; rsgphoto, pp. 4-5; The Florida collection/ Alamy Stock Photo, p. 6; NPS/ Wikipedia, pp. 6-7; Jeffrey Isaac Greenberg 19+/ Alamy Stock Photo, p. 8; dlhedberg, p. 9 (mound materials); Wirestock Creators, p. 9 (palmetto); Tom Fawls, p. 9 (cypress logs); Daniel Wilson/ Alamy Stock Photo, p. 9 (chickee); Bettmann/ Getty Images, p. 10; Angel Wynn/ NativeStock, p. 11; North Wind Picture Archives/ Alamy Stock Photo, p. 12; WINDN/ AP Images, p. 13; PhotoStock-Israel/ Alamy Stock Photo, p. 14; Sandi Smolker, p. 15; Luis M. Alvarez/ AP Images, pp. 16-17; Roberto Galan, p. 17; Turks, p. 18; Mike Dot, p. 19; ZAK BENNETT/ Getty Images, p. 20 (traditional Seminole necklace); Jeffrey Isaac Greenberg 16+/ Alamy Stock Photo, p. 20; The Charles and Valerie Diker Collection of Native American Art/ Wikipedia, p. 21; Sun Sentinel/ Getty Images, p. 22; Ianaré Sévi/ Wikipedia, pp. 22-23; J. PAT CARTER/ AP Images, p. 23; Nativestock Pictures, p. 24; Paulm1993, p. 25; William Silver/ Alamy Stock Photo, p. 26; Octavio Jones, p. 27; NurPhoto/ Getty Images, p. 28 (around 1500); Daniel Korzeniewski, p. 28 (around 1910); Sandral/ Wikipedia, p. 29 (1962); Jeff Greenberg/ Getty Images, p. 29 (1990); winterbilder, pp. 28-29.